FAMILY and LOVE POEMS

Joseph Cashman

978-1-915502-51-3 © 2023 Joseph Cashman

All rights reserved. No part of this book may be reproduced, stored in a retrieval system, or transmitted by any means, electronic, mechanical, photocopying, recording or otherwise without written permission from the author. Published in Ireland by Orla Kelly Publishing. Cover image by the author.

Orla Kelly Publishing
27 Kilbrody,
Mount Oval,
Rochestown,
Cork,
Ireland.

This book is dedicated to the beauty in life

Acknowledgments

I offer sincere thanks to my family, friends and all who contributed directly and indirectly in bringing my collection of poetry to print.

With a special word of thanks to Susan, my family and Orla Kelly for their unwavering support. Again, this book is a cooperative creation. I am deeply grateful to all who contributed and helped in their own unique way in placing the book in your hands.

About the Author

Joseph lives in County Waterford and enjoys walks in nature, sports of all kind and writing. Many of the poems in this book are inspired by the beautiful surrounding local areas and his family.

Contents

Serenade	1
Ever Present Love	2
Lives Together	4
Family on the Sand	5
Circle of Love	6
Company of Family	8
New Love	9
Human Family	10
Family Love and Fidelity	12
Family Beneath the Stars	14
Love of a Thousand Years	16
Blossoming Love	18
Rainbows Rounds	20
Seas of Stars	22
Love of other	24
On the Land they Love	25
Eternity of their Love	26
Nature's Family	27
Divine's Family	28
Familes in Time	30
Lakeshore	32
Forever Love	34
Family of Humanity	36
Waves of Love	38
Rivers of their Love	40

Seeing Love	41
On the Wings of Love	42
Body's Families	44
Forever More	46
Love Reigning	47
Love Beckons	48
Journey Home to Love	50
Eternal Love Divine	52
Subtle Joy and Love	53
Two Hearts in Love	54
Two Families and the Divine	56
Our Family Home	58
Chimes of Divine's Love	60
Other Books by the Author	62

Serenade

Songbirds herald the rising sun
When day is nigh upon the starlit sky
While robin hops upon the window cill
To gaze and chirp to those within
Where couple relax before morning meal.

Resting easy on nearby stove
Whose welcome nurturance
Mirror their loving glances
Of special time together
In hearth and home
Beside a roaring fire.

Whose flame dances
On the reflection of their eyes
To serenade a love renewed.

Fulfilling promises made
Long, long ago
By their hearts and souls
On the shorelines of eternity.

To find each other once again
And keep their love within their care
To blossom forth with unending grace
Through all of time as a love fulfilled.

Ever Present Love

They stood beside each other with a grace profound
And softly spoke to one another with genteel ease
Till their time came to sit and chat about their care
With loving glances and respectful pause,
For each other's turn to talk.

That blessed the space between them as each spoke
And asked about their child's happiness
While every subtle glance of their eyes
Allowed each other time to think
And space to feel and talk
About their loved one.

Which was watched with awe by those present there
That saw the beauty of their caring and deep love
For one another and those they reared
And nothing was left unsaid within the sharing space
Of their loving respectful ways
And genuine love for each other.

While their genteel ease and caring conversation
Seemed to fill the very air and atmosphere
With their deep and respectful love
That every listening heart there
Never forgot what a deep profound
And genuine love felt like, to those who saw
As they both shared their thoughtful cares.

And every atom in the space
Seemed filled with grace
Of a love so deep its depths
Transcend the reach of time
To express a love sublime.

That when reflected on fill the heart and soul
With the belief that all is possible within a love
That so effortlessly creates the space for both to blossom.

And return unspoken gestures across to their partner
Who did the same with no thought of would they care
As care and love for each other blessed the space
That was lovingly given for each word
And time to pause and hear
What the other had to say.

That when pondered on moves the mind
To wish for all the very same partnership
So love can flourish in the simplest days.

And before they stand to say goodbye
Each are touched by the presence of their love
To ne'er forget what they saw before their eyes
And felt with listening heart and soul,
Their deep and ever present love.

Lives Together

Serendipity slides through
The doors of time
From Heaven's holding place
And spirals into life
With exquisite synchronicity.

And spread its holy wings
To share its grace profound
From a timeless space
Prepared with symphonic harmony
Whose chords are built with love.

As love spirals
And lovers meet
To bring their souls
To each other.

And all the music is undone
To begin their symphonies again
As grace pours
Its serendipity anew
Upon the union of their souls.

And pours its life
Upon their hearts
To bring their lives together.

Family on the Sand

Harmonies of sound echo along the shore
From washing foaming waves rolling on the sand
And flighted seagull calling in the sky above
Sharing its joy and summer happiness
With those who happen by or resting there
That fill human heart and mind with open calm.

While distant tinkling sounds on shore and sky
Wash oe'r the beach to join the harmonies
Of voices calling back to family on the sand
As bodies wade gleefully through lapping waves.

That soak into the very core of olden memories
Of carefree summer days beside the sea
Till time back on beach to savour Earth's bounty
Where food is tasted with wet and sandy hands
While every morsel touch the taste buds memory
Of family time together beside the warm sea.

And accompany family on their journey home
While sea's echoing soothing sounds
Linger till journey's end and setting sun beckons,
All to sleep beneath the tinkling light of stars.

Until morning's sounds and smiles
Filling breakfast's gentle conversations
While every rested voice soothes,
Body with calm for a brand new day.

Circle of Love

Falling water droplets alight
From floating clouds of laden lakes
That seem to fly on miracle wings
Like bumble bee's defying of gravity's grasp
Never doubting its tiny wings of flight
As it soars among welcoming flowers.

Where earth watches cloud's zooming droplets
Splash upon emerging plants and flowers
And trickle silently beneath the waiting soil
To nurture root's every cell with cloud's gifts
Who promises to send back what transpires
To the heavens to birth new floating clouds
Completing nature and sky's circle of love.

That is mirrored across all of Earth's home
Through sun's gaze and starlight's rise
Where rays of day are cooled by night
And night's cold hand is warmed by morn sun
To season's bloom in awakening spring
And rest time beneath winter skies
In earth, sun and season's circle of love.

While many a circle awaits completion
In humanity's shared days and stories
Through gentle caring welcomed acts
Of receiving to give and receive again.

Oft' times unexpectedly filled with joy
And blessed with a gratitude returned
To complete a humanity's circle of love.

And seas wash sand upon the shores
For new baby turtles to softly walk upon
As waves wash slowly in to meet them
And wash out again to take them home
To swim within waters of the seven seas
Where sea and shore share a circle of love.

Company of Family

Grass leaves shining with emerald hues
Grow just for fun and become a home
For grasses friends, flowers and more
On every continent across the Earth.

While all of nature, life and human bask
On it's warm summer leaves in the sun
And many a childhood game is played
On its soft surface with friends and pets
Who bark and meow with pure glee
And love of fun just for the sake of joy
On a day with human friends fulfilled.

And many a summer's day is blessed
By the company of family and the sun
Where grass waits for them to play
Upon its soft green carefree leaves.

Until time to pause for awhile
And lay a light cloth down
To rest a meal of Earth's bounty
On a table of grass supporting all
For family to savour special time
Where talk and joy are shared by all
While all's wishes are fulfilled.

New Love

All new memories awaken
And touch the chords of the heart
As two meet on fated path
Where new love begins.

While their gentle love and sharing
Create new dreams to be fulfilled
Within the light of deepening understanding
As each speak the joy of simple sharing
And see the beauty in giving freely;

Without expectation of a gift returned
To birth new ways for their love
Nurtured to fruition by words that care
And hearts that believe in loving deeply.

That blossoms in surprising moments
Where hands of time count no hours
As their newly emerging love
Floats afresh on present time
To greet dreams being fulfilled.

And all that comes before them
On life's many and various paths
Blend with their love and dreams
To bless their lives with endless ease.

Human Family

Everyone is uniquely different
Though from the same human family
And if there were twenty billion of us
Living across our beautiful earthly home
Or spread among the many sentient worlds
Of our vast Milky Way spiralling galaxy home
We would still be uniquely and beautifully different.

Because every cell in our human body
Is created by the Divine with infinite generosity
Who blessed every one of human body's cells
With endless levels of diversity and creativity
Through millions of tiny, tiny filaments
Some connected and others just connecting now
As the awakening millions of filaments line up.

Where our light-activated linking filaments
Form many new spiralling paired DNA strands
Linking and lighting up and, coming back online
And letting us know that we were always made
To be a Divine's magnificent
Light and creativity filled human creation
Gifted to us eons ago and now reawakening

Bringing us to realisation's door
That our great gift to one another
Is to share our Divine given individuality.

And stand as shining stars of lighted information
In a human body of infinite creative potential
Awaiting our awareness of the reawakening
Of millions of filaments and many DNA strands
Connecting now in solid and light forms
And opening codes of light and creativity.

Birthing our
Divine's given gifts and glory
To share with our human family
And beautiful blessed Earth.

Family Love and Fidelity

And all is prepared
In love's domain
To welcome in
Family, love and fidelity
To hearth and home.

As the light shines
High upon the heavens
And my love and I
Hold hands to greet
The beginning
Of a new day dawned.

And every sup
We drink from our cup
Is laden with love Divine
As family sit
Side by side.

Where nurturance
Is shared with all
In home's new hearth
Whose base is built
On family, love
And fidelity.

Family beneath the Stars

Family beneath the stars are infinitely blessed
By Earth our family home and shining sun
As our home gently turns night skies to sun's rays
Awakening earth's sleeping lands to their rising dawn
While we all sail softly through infinite space.

And every balming breath we breathe
Is provided for by our precious and loving earthly home
As her nature's family kingdoms pour oxygen's elixir out
To fill breathing lungs with the breath of life
Who joyfully return their gift of carbon di.

That when reflected on amaze the mind
And reason too, of our family home's ingenuity
Where every gift is shared in circular harmony
Throughout nature's family kingdoms.

Where lakes, rivers and seas water's
Are filled with the gift of oxygen
For some fish families
To swish through their amazing gills
Where grateful capillaries of blood pick up the oxygen.

And everywhere we look or cast a glance
Is filled with endless beauty unparalleled
From airborne soaring wings on sky
To spider's morning gossamer web
Filled with the dancing light of stars.

And sometimes we ponder who cares for all
From the beating living heart of our earthly home
Whose nature's lungs feed us with oxygen
To every sound and breeze across the senses
That let us know that our sentient Earth is alive
And filled with infinite beauty across land and sky above.

Where clouds soak multicolours in
From sun's evening skies high above
As its cooling rays wave so long till morn
While dusk beckons us to settle down
Slowly, to sleep within the boundless beauty
Of Earth our family home beneath the stars.

Love of a Thousand Years

They walked the land in olden days
And ne'er forgot the love they shared
That travels into present day memories
Of trips on sturdy sailing boat and trusted horse
Who carried them to their first meet and eyes embrace
Of a love their hearts and souls brought into being.

And all saw their love for one another
As each loving glance spoke a thousand words.
While they travelled with those who knew
Their love was meant to be for all of time
And every task and role they performed
Was done with a genuine knowing humility;

That their lives were blessed by a love sublime
As they shared their time and kindness
On their many travels across the land
Of the people's kingdom they loved.

While everyone who crossed their path
On their journeys through the vales and plains
And fabled isle with gentle hill and vistas wide
Spoke of their love for each other and the land.

As they met and listened to young and old
In the people's kingdom brimming with benevolence
And when the time came to join their hands
Every couple in the land wished them well.
While memories of their love for each other
Linger over waves of centuries to present times
Where those that still remember their love of yore
Talk about their fated future meeting and destiny
When their lives and love would meet again.

On a land that hold their stories dear
And recall histories and memories
Of their love and kindness in olden days
On the land they loved and ne'er forgot
That were filled with apple gardens to tide's shore
And golden plots of corn beside pastures green.

Where time's centuries reach across
To bring their fated destiny to present times
As the earth feel their footsteps echo softly
Within the fabled isle, vales, plains and shores
While their hearts and souls meet again to embrace
And renew their love of a thousand years
On the land of people's kingdom they love.

Blossoming Love

As the days speed softly away
From the meeting of their souls
Two hearts hold all in their loving care.

While every glance of their deepening love
Is bedecked with loving memories
And every embrace is fully felt
In the deep rivers of their heartbeats.

And those in their care bask in the warmth
Of their caring conversations and shared joy
While every space is filled with their respectful love
In a home built for nurturance
And each other's happiness.

As both their souls hold life's mysteries
Within the palm of gentle strength
And feeling hearts that love deeply
While wishing the very same for all.

Where time has no say over hearts that love
And live their gentleness every day
As both hold each other's dreams
Within the bosom of their souls
And deepest wishes within the safety
Of their blossoming love.

Rainbows Rounds

Love of Earth our family home is a precious gift
That bless our lives in many ways across our day
With special fleeting moments and memories
As our earth unveils its boundless beauty
Across the land and endless skies above.

Where many a special fleeting moment
Is seen on earth's vast daytime skies
As we gaze in wonderment to the heavens
At the ever-changing shape of clouds
And their floating fluffy coloured coats
As they float serenely on wings of wind
Across the heavenly skies above
Where there is a home for every cloud.

While shading earth's sun drenched surface
With a cooling canopy from summer's sun
As cloud's gifts of dropping water droplets
Soar down on wafting wings of joy
To their earthly friends far below
Replenishing land, nature and water reservoir.

And as they soar down from cloud's home
They bless the sky in between cloud and earth
As sunlight's rays of speeding light
Pass through the dropping water droplets
Where rainbow curves softly bloom.

Setting the heavenly skies ablaze
With rainbow curve's of coloured light
That reach and touch the soil below
Where its glistening ends bathe the land
With coloured light and much, much more.

And many a rainbow is greeted in the sky
By one or more rainbow coloured friends
As the Divine rains rainbow rounds from above
While all marvel at the beauty
Of Divine's curves perfect symmetries
And coloured rays of shining light.

Opening heart, mind and soul
To the beauty of the earth and skies above
As we stand upon our blessed Earthly home
Where creation is replenished afresh
With cloud's wafting waters of life
And coloured rainbow curves of Divine.

Seas of Stars

Seas of stars bedeck the sleeping lands
And twinkle until arriving morning's light
Seeming to disappear in daylight's gaze
But Earth's other half in night-time land
Knows the stars are twinkling there
And never doubts starlight's gaze
Shining upon Earth's night sky.

Where they shine their light from afar
And pass between the clouds to all below
To say hello and leave their calling card
That reminds, we have never left
We are always here and to let you know
That the stars and Earth are forever friends.

And as we gaze at the starlit skies
On Divine's sparkling shimmering dome
We step along the rays of twinkling light
And journey to distant stars so numerous
That we could spend countless lifetimes
Numbering the nameless ones.

Bringing us to realisation's door
That as we reflect upon the endless stars above
We touch Divine's great gift to our human family
That blesses everyone with daylight's star
And night-time seas of stars

Love of other

Love of other
Is a special grace
That sits on high
Above the heart.

And beckon home
The souls that meet
To know each other
As partners do.

While their circle
Weaves the glory
Of each other
As all the while
Their circle grows
Upon the stairway
Of the heavens.

And all who see
Their circle know
The weaving of their souls
Who sing the glory
Of each other.

As hearts embrace
Their partnership
To complete the circle
Of their love.

On the Land they Love

A rose's many facet heart
Awakes from a timeless sleep
To unfold upon it's destiny
In timeless synchronicity.

And every hue
Of rose's many facet heart
Is built with love
That beckons forth
The blooming of a rose.

In remembrance
Of its Creator's hand
Whose seed was sown
In Edenic soil
With boundless Love
And Light Divine
Upon the fertile plains
Of Avalon.

Where every wish comes home to rest
Within a golden sunlight fresh
Upon the lands of Eden fair.
As two hearts join as One
In sacred symphony
And wedded harmony
On the land they love.

Eternity of their Love

And all around serene sounds
Of symphonies in harmony
Are aglow with the exquisite grace
Of their love Divine.

That flows in perfect unison
Upon the balcony of their souls
And all that comes before them
Blends their love and light
In perfect symmetry.

To bless the reunion of their souls
As hands are held
In eternal knowing
To don the wedding ring
Of divine alignment
For ever more.

As all their love
Flows into one
To begin again
As life renewed.

And every heartbeat
Comes home to rest
Upon the eternity of their love.

Nature's Family

On nature's family landscapes
Of limitless beauty and benevolence
All are nurtured by it's carefree easy charm
From busy bees to swaying grasses
And flowers that bless the eye and scent.

As they blossom from dawn of morn'
Till starlight's twinkling lights appear
While sun slides below horizon's line
To rise and shine anew at dawn of day.

While every wind oe'r land and water
Bless nature with heavenly sounds
From Divine Creator's skies above
That weave a shimmering symphony.

Across nature's family's home
And air up to soaring dome
That join Earth, skies and nature's family
Together as forever friends.

Divine's Family

An all new dawn has now arisen
And lo behold the beauty born
From morning's rising light
Wrapped in the warmth
Of Divine's caring Love.

That guides us around our sun
As Earth awakens to new dawn rays
On starlight's celestial skies
That beckons a glance to the heavens
Where Divine's created universe
Surrounds our earthly home.

While Divine's loving gaze
Keeps our Sun's solar system
In perfect spiral harmony
With all our spiral families
And the centre of our galaxy
While we all journey together
Across vast cosmic skies.

With our many galaxy families
And our very own universe
That touch the outer edges
Of surrounding universes
On nearby multiverse's skies
And links all Divine's family.

Families in Time

Families in time exist across the cosmic multiverses
And some are visible on our universe's starlit skies
Wherein lies a link that connects
From our present moment
To the present moment of all our families in time
Across the endless multiverse skies.

Where every present moment points towards
All our present moments connecting with each other
Through this very special connecting link
And joins all our present moments on a common time line.

To bring about the meeting
With all our families in time
Who knew we would make the connection
Through this very special connecting link
Where our families in time across the cosmic multiverses
Watched our fated meeting connecting moment,
At this very special connecting link in time.

That connects all present moments, probabilities and possibilities
Now, on a common time line
And a meeting line for all our family worlds
Where every wish cast in the present moment
Is now linked on a common time line
To envision as one entire multiverses family into being.

Across the multiverses many dimensions and realities
And connects all journeys of our families in time
Within the one common time line forever more,
From our sun's seven sister star Pleiadean suns
To galaxy Andromeda's millions of shimmering stars
And all the worlds and, stars across the infinite multiverses.
As we journey home with our galaxy of birth
To Heaven's shores and home of birth
With all our many families, galaxies and multiverses in time.

Lakeshore

On the lakeshore lies a place of beauty
Beckoning the busy heart to rest there
Beside lake's calm soothing waters
Mirroring blue skies and drifting clouds
That seem to go forever on its surface
While water's silence echo the soft notes
Of nesting water fowl in hidden homes
And chirping baby chick's loving call.

As nearby tree's reaching branches create a canopy
For those who rest beneath beside the lakeshore
To soak every pore with all the beauty there
As scent of water reed fill the senses
With peace to soothe their every care.

And lakeshore's ebbing waters remind,
That its ripples move slowly as the sun
Over warm dry pebbles at the waterline
Where birds sip quietly to wet their thirst
And fly away again to family in the sky
As lake cast their reflection on the water
A perfect mirror of their flight high above.

While family bask beneath summer's sun
At lake's oasis far from busy sea
Where shoreline keeps a special place
For family sharing carefree moments.

While hidden surface streams
Send their bounty to lake's home
Cooling the air resting on its shores
And lovingly refreshing water and everyone.

Forever Love

Hills of Taran shores wave softly in the wind
Passing through their soaring hillside trees
And every heart that stands upon its shores
Feel blessed to see their olden home from home
Reaching the fullness of its beauty on days like today
While the brilliant blue light that shines high above
Reflects the light of a newborn Taran eon.

As horses side by side carry two to their destiny
Between low-lying hills to Camelot towering castles
On trail that was often trod eons before
As they glance across to each other's eyes
That know their journeys have not been in vain
Across the stars far from home's place of birth
To the hills of Taran shores
Where their forever love first began.

While old fables that stood the test of time
And foretold the meeting of their hearts and souls
On hills of Taran shores and fabled earthen isle
Are now shimmering on floating flags
Upon highest Taran castles towers on gentle slopes.

As shining trumpets tall echo across cosmic skies
Heralding the joining of their hearts and souls
On Taran hills and fabled earthen isle
Shimmering in the light of a new eon dawn.

That weave their ancient stories to completion
On Earth and Taran lands in present times
And fulfill their destiny on lands they love
Joining Earth and Taran worlds forever more
Whispered about on ancient starlit stairways
And hallowed halls of Heaven's worlds.

While the light of our universe's new eon dawn
Rises across its many stars and galaxies
Where all called for this special time
When everyone would journey home
On cosmic skies in full unity and harmony
Upon the land of their galaxy of birth
And then onto Heaven's shores.

Family of Humanity

Lands in harmony reach down to the sea
That flow up to their shores
And take their harmony across the waves
To their nearest neighbour's lands
Who never wonder why a land's hand
Is reached out for genuine harmony
As they link in friendship across land and sea.

Instantly flowing waves of harmony
Over the sea to nearest neighbour's land
Joining lands and people in harmony and friendship
That rise up to towering mountain ranges
And flow down across hills and valleys of the Earth.

Where each land and people's welcome
Tell a new story of harmony and friendship
While all life across their lands
Send waves of joy soaring in the air
As every creation of the Divine
Hears an echoing call for harmony.

And genuine caring friendship's hand
While maintaining their sovereign rights
On every land, country and family of humanity
Throughout our beautiful earthly home.

Waves of Love

Divine's call echoes across the courtyard
From higher heavenly towers, heralding
All beacons are now lit along the way
For Divine's higher heavenly realms
Journey from above to Earth below.

Travelling on sweeping waves of Divine's love
While singing songs in praise of Earth and life
As the higher heavenly realms reach the Earth
And speed across land and foam
To all life, humanity and every earthly kingdom;

From Earth's surface down to its core below
Where Divine's higher heavenly realms
Send an echoing call across the cosmic skies
Heralding, Divine's full return to Earth and humanity.

On the wings of Divine's instant time
Travelling the cosmic highways of Divine's love
To all of Earth's and humanity's many galaxy families
On countless universes across the multiverses.

Who return their instant and joyful echoing reply
Across the cosmic skies to Earth and humanity
Where every atom of Earth and human cell
Know the echoing call was heard
As all are filled with waves of sound
From galaxies of stars ringing bells.

Pealing their memories and recall
Of Earthly kingdoms shining beauty
And humanity's welcoming hand
As they recall their ageless friendship
Through countless eons and histories
Echoing along the corridors of time.

While the higher heavenly realms sacred sounds
And Divine's symphonies
Bless Earth and humanity
With Divine's infinite love and light
And arise memories in stone laying on the land
That now begin to sing the songs of long ago
As their music awakens to be fulfilled.

Filling all Earth and humanity with the soft tones
Of higher heavenly realms sacred sounds
And symphonies of Divine's love and light

That join lands, sea and stars once again
And Earth, humanity with our many galaxy families
While Earth's kingdoms reawakening remembrance
Connect with the Divine, Earth, humanity and galaxies
And the infinite love and light of Divine's higher heavens.

Rivers of their Love

Benign grace flows through
All the rivers of their love
And lands ashore
On the solid ground
Of fidelity.

While every expression
In their love's terrain
Is filled with exquisite joy
And love sublime
That enfolds it's loving arms
Around their new relationship.

And every ship
Comes home to berth
From eons of journeys forth
To rest upon
The shores of their newfound love.

Where every patchwork quilt
Is now fully sewn into one
To blanket the land
Of their love
With Heaven's help
From Divine domain
To join their hands and hearts
For ever more.

Seeing Love

On the journey of life
There may be, no surprise more blessed
Than seeing love through one's eyes
Where a fleeting sense of peace
Descends upon the heart and mind
And uplifts the soul to higher heights
Oft' times dissolving limitation's story
From steps across the land of hope.

And sometimes awareness of the gift of faith
That sees the blessings of believing
In daring to believe in love
And care about the feelings there.

That join the hands of faith and hope
And builds a new bridge between them
Moving heart and mind to greater harmony
And connection to soul's higher heights
As they dare to dream and believe
That probable can become possible

Where new beginnings and shared dreams
Appear along the path to possible
As all stand together on the horizon of belief.

On the Wings of Love

On the wings of love
My love swoops in
With graceful ease
That carries her love
In divine delight.

And comes ashore
To our hearts
And home's domain
To join our hands
In love and fidelity.

Where every wish
Sweeps across the threshold
And comes home to rest
In our home blessed
And built anew for family.

That lights the hearth
With everlasting love
And blossoms forth
From our hearts entwined.

To fill each space
With the joy and love
Of family, love and fidelity.

Body's Families

Body's families are Divine's priceless given gifts
Who support each other when called upon
And none are considered more important than the other
As all were created to live in complementary harmony.

While some of body's families are seen in solid form
Where hands and feet are supported by the eyes
While other families lie beneath the skin
But yet are treasured body family members
Like beating heart who pumps the blood
Around the body even when we sleep.

And each family seems to have their own intelligence
Like body's millions of tiny cells
Where each cell is filled with many worlds
From nucleus to mitochondria with sparkling cristae
That share their space with cell's Divine given filaments
Who link together creating DNA strands
And talk to each other across their lighted links
Sending information to the nervous system's highways.

While some body families are so subtle
That rainbow colours are their calling card
Such as body's softly spinning circles of energy
Some call chakras and others call receivers of information
Where each spin a rainbow colour on body's centre line
From red, orange, yellow, green, blue, indigo and violet.

Who talk to each other
And share information back and forth with one another
Through emotions, feelings, intellect and higher mind
And also connect to the nervous system highways
Providing other body families with chakra's information
To be translated by body's many senses and intelligences
From the knowing, intuitive, feeling heart
To the receptive, reasoning families of mind
Birthing a new way of being
As many body families become the best of friends.

And many a chakra spins best in calm spaces
As body walks away from jarring sounds
That stagnate their healthy spinning state
And block their information to body's other families.

Where all rests within a sparkling spherical body
That links to Divine's infinite light of information
And our beautiful spherical earthly home
While all body's many, many families
Are blessed by the infinite love of Divine.

Forever More

All is now aligned for ever more
And all the leaves
Are swept aside
On the path to love.

As two hearts
Merge into one
Love for life.

And robin heralds
A new dawn come
In a future ever bright.

As all the sacred
Comes home to rest
Upon their hearts
And light-filled eyes.

Where promises
Blend into one
Eternal love.

As heartfelt wishes
Are fulfilled
By the sacred and Divine
To find a home
Within their hearts forever more.

Love Reigning

All is happening now
As every gateway of the Divine
Has opened wide and cleared the way
For Divine Love reigning on the firmament.

Fulfilling all promises made eons ago
By the Divine and our cosmic families
To our earthly home and humanity
That we would never be alone again
On cosmic skies at galaxy's end.

While soul's longings and heart's belief
Is graced with the clear and sure knowing
That Divine's promises are now fulfilled
Creating a bright present and new future.

As soaring hearts throughout the earth
Welcome the full return of Divine's Love
Making Earth, humanity and all life's
Leap to Divine's Love permanent.

Love Beckons

Love beckons at dawn of fated meeting day
Two hearts that journeyed from afar
To place their feet upon the lighted path of destiny
Dancing across their now awakening lands
And embrace their love's shining dreams
That wished for deepest love with their mirror soul
Who reflects the very same embrace of love.

And as their hearts and souls embrace their love
Shining dreams now fulfill
Across the landscapes of their love's lighted lands
Where every glance touch their souls tenderly.

While every spoken word and hands embrace
Fill the caverns of their hearts with endless love
That shines through every waking moment
As their souls united happiness
Reflects deepest love's highest heights
Within the simplest days of their companionship.

Where outer cares melt away
Beneath the beaming light of love
As hearts beat as one in harmony
And every expression finds a home
Within their souls same embrace of love.

Journey Home to Love

Harmony of mind and thought
Notice in their quiet moments
Deep flowing rivers of emotion
Passing beneath heart's feelings.

That awaken heart's longings
To join in harmony with the soul
And connect with mind and thought
In full unity and harmony.

Arising a new awareness within their memories
As they pause and recall their time with soul
That reach across ancient eons and histories
Here on Earth over millions of years
On the fringes of the Milky Way galaxy.

And reflect upon soul's journey across the stars
From Divine's Heavens to its earthly home
Soul, mind and heart recall ancient memories
Of humanity's longing for all to belong in unity
On Earth, galaxy, universe and multiverse.

Where all now ready for the journey home
To Divine's Home in the Heavens
In the eon of full unity that soul recalls
Is happening now on earth, solar system and galaxy
And across our universe and multiverse
As all unify now for the journey home to love;

Across time, up the spiral links of light and love
Where all Earth and humanity set a course
Up the spiral links of Earth's planet family
To join her Gaian, Taran and Tiamat sister planets
And her many other sisters, suns and galaxies
While connecting with our sun's seven sister Pleiadean suns
That link rainbow bridges of light across the galaxies
And our universe, twelve surrounding universes and
multiverses.

As we all journey home to love
Back through the circular window
Up the spiral links of light and love's vibration
With Earth's sister planets, stars and family galaxies
Fulfilling Divine's longing for all's full safe return
And completes a great quest of all creation
To be within the highest vibration of Divine's Love.

Eternal Love Divine

All the heavens are now aligned
As their love of a thousand eons
And their souls join beyond the veil of time
To a love began beneath the stars of Heaven
And ventured across many worlds and earthen lands
Where they journeyed with each other.

While many a season prepared them for a time
When every beat of both their hearts
Brought them gently closer to that day
When their souls would meet again
Upon the sands of time and earthen shores.

And fill the sands of time with ringing bells and recall
Of a love so deep its depth transcends the reach of time
To touch the timeless realm of eternal love Divine
Sweeping across every glance of their eyes that greet
Each other on the step that brought them home.

Fulfilling all promises made to each other
Within the very heart and halls of time
To be with each other forever more
As they live together on earthen shores
Where their hearts, souls and eternal love Divine
Blend as one for eternity.

Subtle Joy and Love

Subtle joy unfolds endlessly
From the caverns of the heart
And travels on the beat and pulse
Of heart's streams running rivers
Where flutters of joy pour onto life
From the glancing smile of a loved one.

As heart feels the beauty of a smile
And welcome from those it loves
That weave the gift of joy into life
And nurture heart's running rivers
Who knows the joy is always there
To be called upon when we gaze,
On all we care about and love in life.

While the subtle senses of the soul
Gladly shares its subtle love
From its home beside heart
To bless precious time
And day's moments.

And all returns
To the caverns of heart's home
Who gladly shares it's joy with soul's love
Blending both in unison
To be called upon to grace precious moments
And bless life and relationships.

Two Hearts in Love

Love begins anew each day
As the hands of time reach across
Midnight's slumbering threshold
To step upon tomorrow's moment
As time turns to a new day.

While two heart's beat side by side
Where every beat is the beat of love
And speeds o'er the land of twinkling stars
To echo on the shorelines of their souls
Where their resting love is gently tended to.

As they rest beneath the starlit skies
While fresh new dreams are softly dreamt
And overseen by their souls illumined love
Who pour care upon their sleeping calm
To grace moments and beating hearts
Throughout their dreaming, sleeping hours.

And gently calls the awakening moment
Of their dreaming sleeping hearts
At dawn of morning's soft rays
Where old footprints in the sand
Wash away on tides of yesterday
And new dreams appear upon vistas of today
Where each glance fill the windows of their souls
With new love for today's moments.

That weaves a softly glittering silken tapestry
Within the landscapes of their hearts and souls
Until today's loving moments are fulfilled
And day's light gives way till dawn.

As dusk beckons two hearts to rest
Beneath the serene care of their souls
In soft embrace until morning's light
Where their dreams await tomorrow's dawn
To bless two hearts in love day again.

Two Families and the Divine

Family of human self is lovingly surrounded
By family of highest soul self above and the Divine
Who connect to heart, mind and soul of human self
Whose every request sent above
Is received and listened to lovingly
And nothing is forgotten or cast aside
By family of highest soul self and the Divine.

And when awareness of family above
Clothes every request from human self
Mountains move aside in between
Clearing the way for communication
And renewing friendship always there.

That open new pathways of receptivity
Within heart, mind and soul of human self
For love and gifts to flow from above
Where every gift is lovingly prepared
By highest soul self's family and the Divine.

As they weave a silken tapestry of reply
Woven with beauty beyond compare
Down to the finest minutest detail
And lovingly created and prepared
To meet seamlessly moment to moment
Before the gifts are sent with infinite love
From family of highest soul self and the Divine.

That when reflected upon
Moves the mind to see the miracle
Of how every gift is placed with care
Within moments of each day.

While space is cleared and swept clean
For tomorrow's gifts to be placed upon
The moment the request is sent above.

Awakening an awareness in the self
That knows human self family's love
Is fully supported with infinite love from above
By highest soul self's family and the Divine.

Joining the two families and the Divine
Within the human heart, mind and soul
Who realise that we are always loved
Throughout each day and every night
Of life's journey.

Our Family Home

Timeless beauty spreads it's broad wings
Over our family home among the stars
As Earth's blue dome bless the heavens
With Earthly creation's infinite beauty
Reaching back over millions of years.

And every sojourn of the Divine
Blessed life placed on its lands and seas
While Earth's shining beauty beyond compare
Blossomed fully in the hands of the Divine
And now every facet of earth's shining jewel
Shimmers as a light-filled star of Divine
Across its galaxy's spiralling arms.

And reflects out to our cosmic families
To say we are here and love you too
As soul remembers it's home from home
On a galaxy far across many heavenly galaxies
Who remind soul, they too remember
And never forgot our earthly home
A shining jewel of timeless beauty.

Chimes of Divine's Love

Chimes of Divine's Love
Emanate from the heart of the Divine
And travel on Divine's light
To descend from starlit skies
And gently alight with graceful ease
On Earth's beating heart and core below.

Where Earth's heart and core hear the sounds
Of chiming love from the Divine
Resounding through every atom and cell
Awakening now across all her kingdoms
As earth rebuilds her pillars of sound and light
Within and upon earth's vast domains
On every level from core to ground above.

That weave a web of sound and light
Upon all lands around the Earth
And rolling seas, lakes and rivers too
While all creation join as one in unison
In a seamless web of endless harmony.

And create chiming waves of harmony
Within the beating heart and core of earth
That link all her pillars of sound and light
On the standing waves of chiming love
In perfect symmetry from core to soil.

Where Divine's waves of chiming love emerge
To travel o'er the surface of the earth
Up to the highways of her soaring dome
While mountain tops chime bells of recall
Clearly heard within humanity's heart.

As Divine's chiming sounds of love bless all
And Earth basks in the chimes of love
While nature blossoms across the land
And softly sways to the sound of chimes
From Earth, Divine and mountain tops.

And every beating heart resounds
In fond recall of Divine's chiming sounds
Wafting gently on the wings of wind
Across every land, sea and rolling foam
To sweep o'er the shores and back to land again.

Where every chime returns to the heart
Of Earth, humanity, all life and Divine's Love
As chiming sounds journey softly home
And join all hearts in harmony forever more.

Other Books by the Author

Introducing 50+2 POEMS Just For You, a unique collection of original poetic works crafted to inspire and awaken the imagination. This special anthology includes over fifty poems covering numerous topics of interest that appeal to all ages.

With thought-provoking and inspiring reflections woven into each work, this delightful collection will bring a smile to your face and captivate you with its vivid imagery.

Each poem is written with emotion and vibrant detail to stir your senses. Let these words soothe your soul - fill your spirit with joy - spark the inner flame that ignites creativity.

Whether you're in need of a bit of personal motivation or want to share an inspiring poem with someone special, 50 + 2 Poems has something for everyone.

So come and enjoy an enchanting journey through each poem and make some magical moments with 50+2 POEMS - Just for You.

DIVINE DESIGN Poetry of the Heart and Soul is a sublime collection of poetry that speaks to the heart and soul. Uncovering the special relationship between the heart, soul and Divine with deep understanding and scintillating clarity. Each poem is a treasure trove of beautiful moments and a freshness that is exhilarating, encouraging us to recognise Divine Design all around us.

Many of the poems in this anthology are filled with wonderful insights taking the reader on a journey of discovery. Moments such as simple acts of sharing with those we love, friends who help us out, or when paths cross just by chance--show that we are always cared for and loved. They also speak of Divine Design soaring over Earth below to bless teeming seas and shores with shoals of fish and fertile waters as well as nature's gardens and landscapes and all creatures who dwell there.

Finally, the book reminds us that our Creator's infinite light and love blesses Earth, all life, and humanity endlessly -- something we can certainly aspire to do ourselves in our daily lives.

This book is perfect for readers wanting to explore how their own lives are blessed through Divine Design. Through its thoughtful writing and exquisite illustrations, readers can share moments of joy, love, abundance, and kindness as they delve into the mysterious depths of Divine Design.

So come and enjoy a journey of heart and soul in this beautiful book of poetry.

www.ingramcontent.com/pod-product-compliance
Lightning Source LLC
Chambersburg PA
CBHW041314110526
44591CB00022B/2910